WORKBOOK FOR
NO TIME TO PANIC
(A Guide to Matt Gutman's Book)

Your Powerful Guide to Curbing Anxiety and Conquering a Lifetime of Panic Attacks

ABOUT MATT GUTMAN

Matt Gutman, who is headquartered in Los Angeles, is the Chief National Correspondent for ABC News. His work has appeared on "World News Tonight with David Muir," "20/20," "Good Morning America," and "Nightline," among other ABC News programs and outlets. He has filed reports from 40 different nations for ABC News.

Gutman, a journalist who has won various awards, has reported on the COVID-19 outbreak, the protests that followed George Floyd's death in the United States, the immigration problem, and numerous terrorist incidents both abroad and at home.

Over the past five years, Gutman has become one of "20/20's" most reliable journalists. Both the "20/20" documentary on the 2017 Las Vegas shooting and the "20/20" Christopher Award–winning coverage of the Thai cave rescue were made possible by Gutman's relentless reporting. Following the perilous rescue of 12 boys and their soccer coach from a flooded cave in Thailand, Gutman was there every step of the way. After the rescue, he wrote "The Boys in the Cave," which told the story of the unlikely heroes among the cave divers, the US Air Force, and the Thai Navy Seals.

His work on the Trayvon Martin shooting and the BP oil spill while he was based in Miami earned him several honors.

He was the host of "Sea Rescue," a children's television program that aired on ABC on Saturday mornings from 2013-2018 and was awarded the Emmy for Outstanding Children's Series in 2016.

Gutman spent seven years as a Jerusalem-based reporter covering every major conflict in the Middle East before joining ABC News in 2008, where he began at ABC News Radio.

Gutman has a wife and two children. A product of Williams College in Williamstown, Massachusetts, he has a degree in philosophy.

THIS ONE WEEK OUTLINE WAS DEVELOPED TO HELP YOU.

> ➢ The foremost thing
> is to find a
> person you can rely on to
> help you achieve your

goals if you want to be successful.

➤ Be careful not
to make any mistakes when filling out the vital forms displayed below.

➤ Consider each day's tip, task and prescription carefully.

THINK ABOUT THEM MEDITATIVELY.

➤ Everything you learned in the note should be

written and meditated upon.

Also, jot down your thoughts and feelings, as well as the obstacles you've come to terms with.

READ AND LISTEN TO EVERYTHING THAT IS BEING SAID AND RECOMMENDED.

Without a doubt, adhere to them.

IT WAS MADE TO BE POSSIBLE.

Never doubt the fact that you
can do it, and never give up hope.

YOU'RE ALL SET TO STEP ON TO THE NEXT LEVEL!

Ensure that you fill out the Form below in its entirety.

DATE IT ALL BEGINS

_____

_____

DATE OF FINAL CONCLUSION (Usually 7 D ays from the starting Date)

_____

Fill in the blanks with your name and email address:

_____

_____

FILL OUT YOUR AGE

_____

_____

It's not as difficult as you might
think, but don't take it for granted and keep going.

Recommendations and Tasks for the Day Don't End That Day; Carry On and Make Habits of Them.

<u>DAY 1</u>

INSIGHT

Although overeating has great adverse effect on how long a person lives, it goes unnoticed most of the time. You are obliged to eat barely enough for the moment.

WHAT YOU SHOULD IMBIBE TODAY

Reduce your calorie intake by 10-50% for increase in your maximum lifespan. Doing this reduces excess body weight and belly fat which can also be linked with shorter lifespan, fatigue and depression.

__DON'T FORGET...__

A lessened calorie intake makes the
likelihood of disease less possible to
happen. However, you should know
that this does not imply that you
should starve yourself.

MEDITATE

_____

_____

_____

_____

_____

_____

_____

_____

_____

_____

_____

_____

_____

**Eat just enough to hold you, the
extra is poison!**

DAY 2

INSIGHT

Replacing your processed foods with plant food and more natural diet is among the best ways to increase your maximum lifespan and happy life with great health. Understand that processed food like sugars are not the natural needs of your body, they are indeed slow killers.

WHAT YOU SHOULD IMBIBE TODAY...

Let go of those artificial foods you consume frequently, Begin to eat more vegetables and purely natural dishes. Also use natural leaves and spices to garnish your food. Reduce meat intake as much as possible.

<u>DON'T FORGET...</u>

Most diseases we suffer can be
attributed to these artificial foods
especially cancer and organ disease.

MEDITATE

_____

_____

_____

_____

_____

_____

_____

_____

_____

_____

**These foods pose great
burden to your system.**

<u>DAY 3</u>

INSIGHT

Always being physically active lets you remain healthy. In fact, it has the ability to add up years to your life. Don't practice sedentary lifestyle, stay fit and bubble like fresh wine.

WHAT YOU SHOULD IMBIBE TODAY

Fix in exercises into your daily routine from today. It helps your immune stay capable, it makes you alive.

<u>DON'T FORGET...</u>

Don't jeopardize exercising, even for
one day!!!

MEDITATE...

_____

_____

_____

_____

_____

_____

_____

_____

_____

_____

_____

_____

_____

_____

_____

_____

_____

_____

_____

_____

_____

_____

_____

_____

_____

_____

_____

**Health is wealth, preserve
it by all means.**

DAY 4

25

INSIGHT

Totally keeping off from the intake of alcohol, cigarette or hard drugs is one of the prime practices for living happy, healthy and long.

WHAT YOU SHOULD IMBIBE TODAY

Stay away any form of hard drug, drug abuse, alcohol or cigarette without compromise. Consider it poison capable of sending you to early grave.

__DON'T FORGET...__

.There things don't work for your own
good; they're 'pleasurable killers'.

__MEDITATE__

_____

_____

27

_____
_____
_____
_____
_____
_____
_____
_____
_____
_____
_____
_____

_____
_____
_____
_____

Say no to drugs! Check out what it does to people!!

DAY 5

INSIGHT

Your happiness must at all times remain at the top of your scale of preferences. Stay away from anything that steals your happiness and peace.

WHAT YOU SHOULD IMBIBE TODAY...

Don't regulary mix up with toxic, sad and depressed people so that they don't pass that energy to you. Do things that make you happy, avoid those that don't.

<u>DON'T FORGET</u>

Being happy makes your life sweeter
and better, it makes you live longer.
Don't jeopardize your happiness at
any time..

MEDITATE

_____

_____

_____

_____

_____

_____

_____

_____

_____

_____

_____

_____

_____

_____

_____

_____

_____

_____

_____

_____

_____

_____

_____

_____

_____

_____

_____

Build yourself to the extent that
nothing would be able to rob you of
your joy. You become invincible in
that state.

DAY 6

<u>INSIGHT</u>

Chronic stress, anxiety, lack of sleep or rest should not be practiced by you. Have a life pattern that ensures entirely that these things don't exist in your life.

<u>WHAT YOU SHOULD IMBIBE TODAY</u>

Start to learn how to avoid stress, anxiety and lack of rest or sleep entirely. Don't involve yourself in unimportant and tedious tasks; always have good night rests.

<u>DON'T FORGET</u>

Stress weakens your cells; limited rest
stops them from healing!! Doesn't
this sound like death?

MEDITATE

_____

_____

_____

_____

_____

_____

_____

_____

_____

**Keep off from anything
that'd stress you, ensure
this limited time on Earth.**

DAY 7

<u>INSIGHT</u>

Your social circle has more impact on you than you might ever imagine. Keeping toxic, sad or annoying people around you could drain you of your life!

<u>WHAT YOU SHOULD IMBIBE TODAY</u>

Always review your social network, be with people that strengthen and make you happy.

<u>DON'T FORGET</u>

You don't deserve to spend even a minute with the wrong people, keep them at length.

MEDITATE

_____

_____

_____

_____

_____

_____

_____

_____

_____

_____

_____

_____

Good networks empower, bad ones destroy!

YOU'VE FINISHED WITHTHIS ONE WEEK GUIDE. KEEP UP WITH IT.

POSITIVE RESULT COMES WITH IT.

Show Love to people by giving them copies of this.

_____

_____

_____

_____

_____

_____

_____

_____

_____

_____

_____

_____

_____

_____

_____

BYE!

Each time you're deviating, return to this!

Made in the USA
Las Vegas, NV
21 September 2023

77912401R00024